PILLOW PATCHES
and other possibilites

Nancy J. Smith & Lynda S. Milligan

The Pillows
Photo Pages

Thank You

We would like to thank the following companies for:
Buttons – Gay Bowles Sales, JHB International
Pillow Forms – Fairfield Soft Touch®, Mountain Mist® Pillowloft™
Fabrics – Aptex, Fabric Traditions, United Notions

A special thanks to Jan Albee for the use of her lovely home during photography!

Credits

Sharon Holmes — Editor, Typesetter, Electronic Illustrator
Susan O'Brien — Graphic Designer, Photo Stylist, Electronic Illustrator
Jane Dumler — Sewing Consultant
Brian Birlauf — Photographer

POSSIBILITIES®

Pillows With Stitched-On "Patches"

Use these directions for Garden Posies, Linen Remembrance, Heart 'n Home, Holiday Wrappings, Homespun Christmas, Printed Patches, and Pumpkin Pals. Refer to color photos for placement of appliques and embellishments.

Stitched-On "Patches" – 12" Pillow

Use ¼" seam allowance throughout.

Materials: ⅞ yd. (.8 m) fabric
⅓ yd. fabric for "patch" (front & back)
scraps for appliques
12" pillow form (soft)
fusible web, six ¾"-⅞" buttons

1. Make the basic pillow cover.
   a. Cut fabric 21½"x 26½". Note: If fabric is not sturdy enough, use a lightweight bondable interfacing to line the wrong side before cutting out the fabric.

   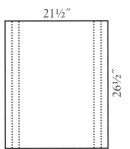

   b. Press 1½" hem to wrong side of one 26½"side of fabric rectangle. Press 1½" to wrong side again, forming a hem of double thickness. Repeat pressing of double hem on other 26½"side of fabric rectangle.
   c. Fold pressed rectangle in half, wrong sides together, with raw edges at bottom. Folded rectangle should now measure 15½"x 13¼".
2. Make the "patch".
   a. For **Garden Posies, Heart 'n Home, Holiday Wrappings,** and **Homespun Christmas,** cut two pieces of "patch" fabric 8½"square. Lay pieces right sides together. Stitch around square, leaving 3"opening along one side for turning. Trim corners, turn, press. Slipstitch opening closed.
   b. For **Linen Remembrance,** cut an 8½"square from old embroidered linen and back it with a piece of muslin as in Step 2a.
   c. For **Pumpkin Pals,** tear an 8½"square of background fabric and fringe the edges about ¼"deep. If pillow cover fabric shows through, back patch with a 7¾"square of lightweight bondable interfacing.
   d. For **Printed Patches,** cut out a motif approximately 8" to 10" from a preprinted panel and back it with a piece of fabric as in Step 2a.
3. Finish the "patch".
   a. For **Holiday Wrappings,** and **Homespun Christmas,** bond designs to "patch" following manufacturer's directions.
   b. For **Garden Posies,** bond designs to "patch" following manufacturer's directions. Make yo-yos from 4" and 6" circles and tack in place.

c. For **Heart 'n Home:**
- **Flag Heart** – Trace heart pattern onto paper. Using the "stitch-on-the-line" patchwork technique, stitch pieces of fabric to paper in order given, right sides together. Cut out the heart shape. Cut backing larger than heart, place right sides together and stitch around entire outside edge. Trim backing, clip. Slit backing in center of heart. Turn. Press. Applique to "patch" with machine blanket stitch. Sew button to star area.

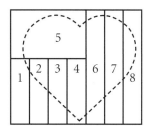

- **House** – Fuse design to "patch". Embellish with buttons.
- **Star** – Fuse design to "patch". Sew button cluster in center.
- **Heart in Hand** – Trace heart onto paper. Stitch strips to heart right sides together in order given. Machine embroider seamlines. Tear away paper. Cut backing larger than heart, place right sides together, and stitch around entire outside edge. Trim backing, clip. Slit backing in center of heart. Turn. Press. Back hand with fusible web and cut out. Cut thumb on line. Place hand on "patch" and slide heart under thumb. Bond. Tack loose edges of heart and add button cluster.
- **Patchwork Heart** – Stitch sixteen 2"squares into a block four squares by four squares. Follow Flag Heart directions to make heart and applique to "patch".

4. Center "patch" on pressed pillow cover. Pin. Stitch in place with one of the following methods.
   a. machine blanket stitch
   b. hand blanket stitch
   c. machine blind hem stitch
   d. hand applique stitch
   e. hand running stitch
   f. machine straight stitch
   g. machine blind hem with clear nylon thread
   h. machine top stitch

   Center "Patch"

5. Open out pillow cover, including pressed hems. Stitch 21½"sides, right sides together, with a ¼"seam allowance. Press seam allowance to one side. Turn pillow cover right side out.
6. Refold and pin pressed hems in place. Stitch each hem close to fold.

7. Make three buttonholes (⅞″ to 1″, depending on button sizes) in top side of each hem, one at the center and one spaced 3″ to either side. Stitch buttons into position under buttonholes. Slide pillow cover over pillow form and button up. (See Alternatives to Buttonholes, page 24.)

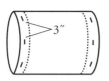

Finishing Details (as photographed)

Garden Posies, Heart 'n Home, and Printed Patches – "Patch" was attached with a hand running stitch using six strands of embroidery floss (or use perlé cotton).

Linen Remembrance – "Patch was hand appliquéd to pillow cover. Extra buttons and ribbons were sewn on the top layer between buttonholes. A button cluster was added.

Holiday Wrappings – Jingle bells were used instead of buttons to close sides of pillow. "Patch" was attached with machine blanket stitch. A ceramic button or jingle bell finished Santa's hat.

Homespun Christmas – "Patch" was attached with machine blanket stitch. Snowman's scarf fringe was made with machine blanket stitch. Blush makeup was used for Santa's and Snowman's cheeks. Old buttons embellished Santa's suit, Snowman's scarf, and the tips of the tree boughs.

Pumpkin Pals – "Patch" was straight stitched to pillow cover ¼″ from the fringe. Ceramic buttons were mixed with regular ones to close sides of pillow, and stars were fused under some of the buttons.

Stitched-On "Patches" – 16″ Pillow

Use these directions for Childhood Memories, Shades of Red, and Warm Fuzzy Flannels.

Use ¼″ seam allowance throughout.
Materials: 1 yd. (1 m) fabric
⅓ yd. (.3 m) fabric for "patch" (front &/or back)
scraps for patchwork & sashing
16″ pillow form (soft)
ten ¾″-⅞″ buttons

1. Make the basic pillow cover.
   a. Cut fabric 25½″ x 34½″. Note: If fabric is not sturdy enough, use a lightweight bondable interfacing to line the wrong side before cutting out the fabric rectangle.

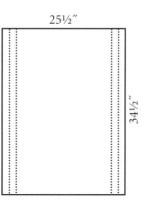

25½″

34½″

b. Press 1½″ hem to wrong side of one 34½″ side of fabric rectangle. Press 1½″ to wrong side again, forming a hem of double thickness. Repeat pressing of double hem on other 34½″ side of fabric rectangle.
   c. Fold pressed rectangle in half, wrong sides together, with raw edges at bottom. Folded rectangle should now measure 19½″ x 17¼″.
2. Make the "patch".
   a. **Childhood Memories** – Have child's photo or artwork transferred to fabric. See photo transfer information on page 7. Cut an 8½″ square from the fabric with the photo transfer centered.
   b. **Shades of Red** – Using scraps, stitch the Basket block. See directions on page 4.
   c. **Warm Fuzzy Flannels** – Using flannel scraps, stitch one of the blocks shown. See directions on page 4.
   Pin block right sides together with a piece of backing fabric cut slightly larger than the block. Pin. Stitch around block, leaving 3″ opening on one side for turning. Trim seams and corners, turn, press. Slipstitch opening closed.
3. Center "patch" on point on pressed pillow cover. Pin. Stitch in place with one of the methods in Step 4 on page 2.

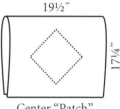

19½″

17¼″

Center "Patch"

4. Open out pillow cover, including pressed hems. Stitch 25½″ sides, right sides together, with a ¼″ seam allowance. Press seam allowance to one side. Turn pillow cover right side out.
5. Refold and pin pressed hems in place. Stitch each hem close to fold.
6. Make five buttonholes (⅞″ to 1″, depending on button sizes) in top side of each hem, one at the center and two placed to either side, all spaced 2″ apart. Stitch buttons into position under buttonholes. Slide pillow cover over pillow form and button up. (See Alternatives to Buttonholes, page 24.)

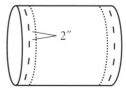

3

Shades of Red

Basket

Finished "patch" is 10″ including sashing
Cut block:

    A. one 8⅞″ square*
    B. one 4⅞″ square*
    C. five 2⅞″ squares*
    D. one 2½″ square

Note: To use more fabrics in a block, cut extra squares of C from different fabrics. Some triangles cut from these squares will be left over.

Cut sashing:

    two rectangles 1½″ x 8½″
    two rectangles 1½″ x 10½″

*Cut A, B, and C squares diagonally into triangles. Piece block in sections as shown.

A, B, C

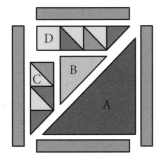

Childhood Memories

Sashed Square

Finished "patch" is 10″ including sashing
Cut sashing:

    four rectangles 1½″ x 8½″
    four 1½″ squares

Piece sashing to photo transfer square in rows.

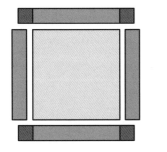

Warm Fuzzy Flannels

Four-Patch

Finished "patch" is 10″ including sashing
Cut for Block 1:

    A. four 4½″ squares

Cut for Block 2:

    A. two 4½″ squares
    B. two 4⅞″ squares*

Cut for Block 3:

    B. four 4⅞″ squares*

Cut sashing for each block:

    four rectangles 1½″ x 8½″
    four 1½″ squares

*Cut B squares diagonally into triangles. You may have leftover triangles. Piece block in rows as shown.

B

Block 1   Block 2   Block 3

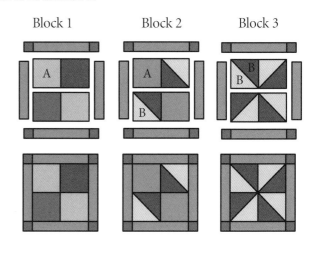

Finishing Details (as photographed)

Childhood Memories – "Patch" was attached with machine blind hem and clear nylon thread.

Shades of Red – "Patch" was attached with machine blind hem and clear nylon thread.

Warm Fuzzy Flannels – "Patch" was stitched to pillow in the ditch created between the block and the sashing. We added novelty buttons.

Pillows With Set-In "Patch"

Use these directions for Amish Simplicity, Country Charm, and Candy Confetti. All are 12″ pillows.

Amish Simplicity or Country Charm

Use ¼″ seam allowance throughout.

Materials: several ⅛ yd. (.2 m) fabric pieces for patchwork
  ⅓ yd. (.3 m) fabric for above & below block
  ½ yd. (.5 m) fabric for pillow cover sides
  12″ pillow form (soft)
  six ¾″-⅞″ buttons

1. Make one of the following patchwork blocks.
2. Cut:
   One piece 3″ x 8½″ for pillow cover below block
   One piece 8½″ x 16″ for pillow cover above block
   Two pieces 7″ x 26½″ for pillow cover sides
3. Stitch as shown. Cover should measure 21½″ x 26½″.

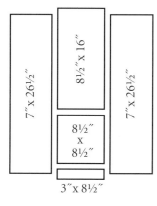

4. Press 1½″ hem to wrong side of one 26½″ side of fabric rectangle. Press 1½″ to wrong side again, forming a hem of double thickness. Repeat pressing of double hem on other 26½″ side of fabric rectangle.
5. Open out pillow cover, including pressed hems. Stitch 21½″ sides, right sides together, with a ¼″ seam allowance. Press seam allowance to one side. Turn pillow cover right side out.

After Pressing Hems
15½″

26½″

Block

6. Refold and pin pressed hems in place. Stitch each hem close to fold.
7. Make three buttonholes (⅞″ to 1″, depending on button sizes) in top side of each hem, one at the center and one spaced 3″ to either side. Stitch buttons into position under buttonholes. Slide pillow cover over pillow form and button up. (See Alternatives to Buttonholes, page 24.)

Square in a Square

Finished "patch" is 8″ including sashing
Cut block:
   A. one 2⅝″ square
   B. two 2⅜″ squares*
   C. two 3″ squares*
   D. two 3⅞″ squares*

Note: To use more fabrics in a block, cut extra squares of B, C, and D from different fabrics. Some triangles cut from these squares will be left over.

Cut sashing:
   four rectangles 1½″ x 6½″
   four squares 1½″ x 1½″

B, C, D

*Cut all B, C, and D squares diagonally into triangles. Piece block by adding triangles around center square as shown.

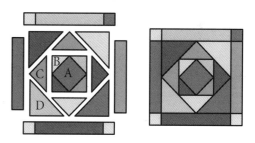

Churn Dash

Finished "patch" is 8″ including sashing
Cut block:
   A. one 2½″ square
   B. four 2⅞″ squares*
   C. eight rectangles 1½″ x 2½″

Note: To use more fabrics in a block, cut extra squares of B from different fabrics. Some triangles cut from these squares will be left over.

Cut sashing:
   four rectangles 1½″ x 6½″
   four 1½″ squares

B

*Cut B squares diagonally into triangles. Piece block in rows as shown.

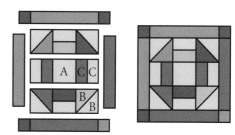

5

Four-Patch

Finished "patch" is 8″ including sashing
Cut block: sixteen 2″ squares
Cut sashing: four rectangles 1½″ x 6½″
              four 1½″ squares
Piece in rows as shown.

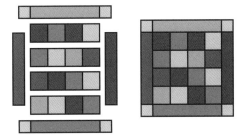

Variable Star

Finished "patch" is 8″ including sashing
Cut block:

    A. one 3½″ square
    B. four 2″ squares
    C. one 4¼″ square*
    D. four 2⅜″ squares*

Note: To use more fabrics in a block, cut extra squares of C and D from different fabrics. Some triangles cut from these squares will be left over.
Cut sashing:

    four rectangles 1½″ x 6½″
    four 1½″ squares

*Cut C square into four triangles.
*Cut D squares into two triangles.
Piece block in rows as shown.

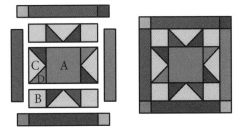

Candy Confetti
Dimensional Pinwheel

Finished "patch" is 8″ including sashing
Fabric: several ⅛ yd. (.2 m) pieces for patchwork
Cut block:

    A. four 3½″ squares of Fabric A
    B. four 3½″ squares of Fabric B

Cut sashing:

    four rectangles 1½″ x 6½″
    four 1½″ squares

Make 4 prairie points with Fabric A squares. Place two prairie points on a Fabric B square, raw edges even, double-folded edges of prairie points fitting tightly together, and pin. Place another Fabric B square right sides together on top of pinned square. Pin, and stitch side. Make another unit the same way. Stitch two units together into block. Add sashing.

To Make Prairie Points

To Make Block

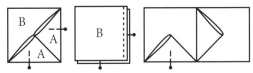

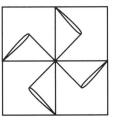

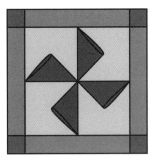

Finishing Details (as photographed)

Amish Simplicity – Very plain flat buttons were chosen to close sides of pillow.
Candy Confetti – Novelty buttons were chosen to close sides of pillow.
Country Charm – A variety of buttons was used.

Other Possibilities

The "patches" used on pillows in this book can be used in many other ways.
Use our list for a take-off point, and let your imagination be your guide!

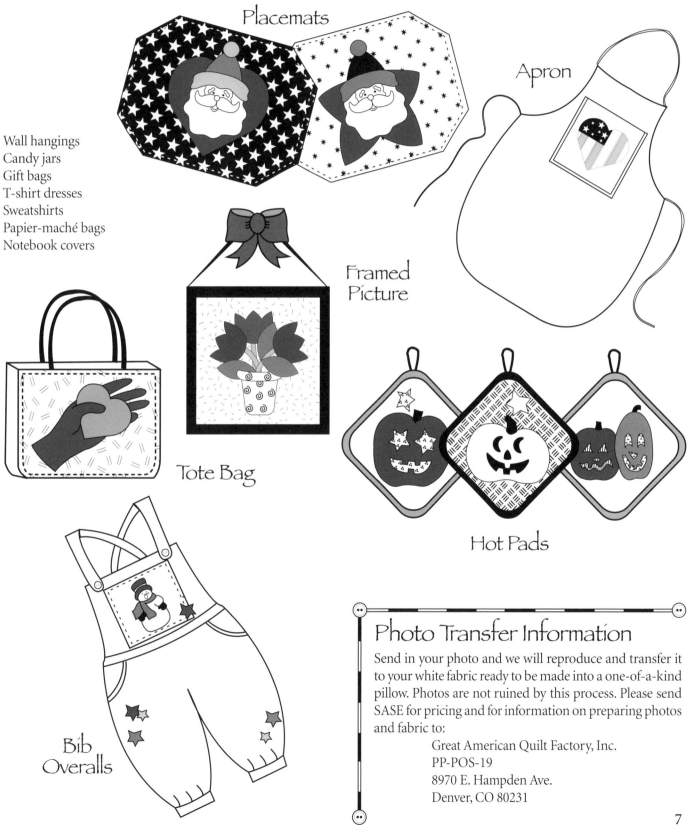

Placemats

Apron

Wall hangings
Candy jars
Gift bags
T-shirt dresses
Sweatshirts
Papier-maché bags
Notebook covers

Framed
Picture

Tote Bag

Hot Pads

Bib
Overalls

Photo Transfer Information

Send in your photo and we will reproduce and transfer it to your white fabric ready to be made into a one-of-a-kind pillow. Photos are not ruined by this process. Please send SASE for pricing and for information on preparing photos and fabric to:

Great American Quilt Factory, Inc.
PP-POS-19
8970 E. Hampden Ave.
Denver, CO 80231

Fabric circle for yo-yo is cut 6″

Garden Posies

Tulip patterns are given in reverse, so there is no need to trace the stems in reverse to make them appear as they do in the photos.

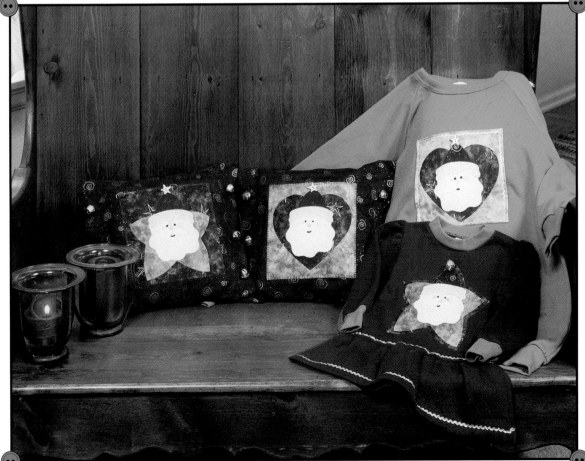

CANDY CONFETTI

Doll patterns from DreamSpinners® — K.T. & Company #156, Little Bits #167

AMISH SIMPLICITY

Fabric circle for yo-yo is cut 6″

Garden Posies

Fabric circles for yo-yos are cut 4″

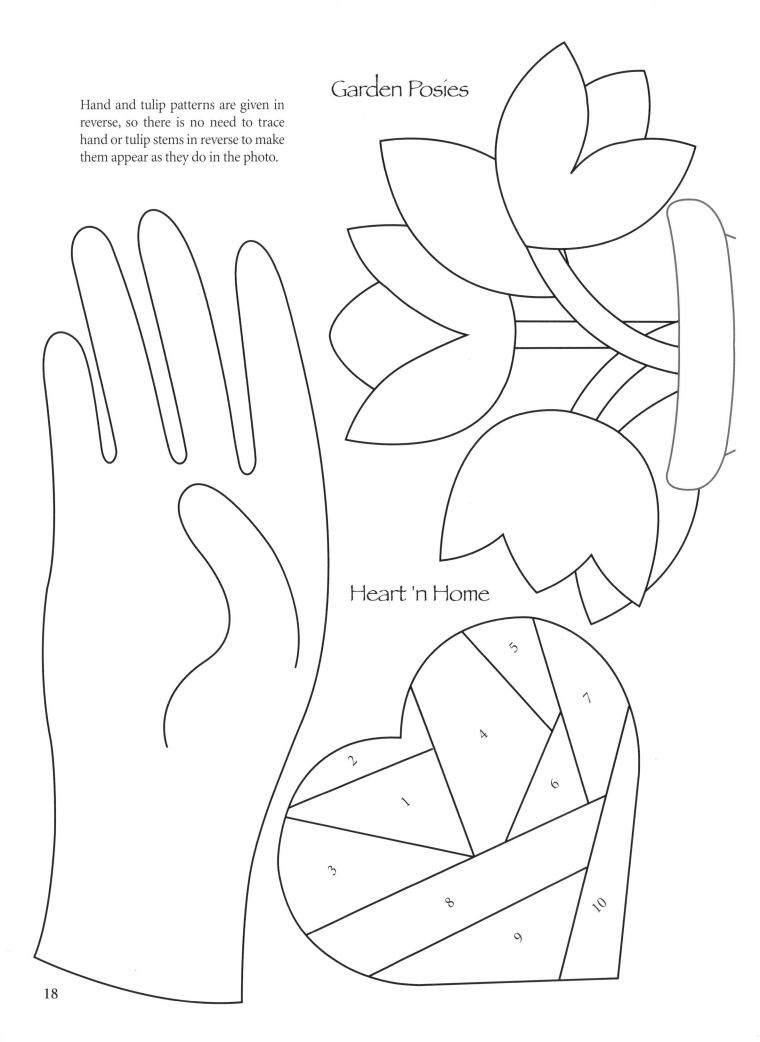

Hand and tulip patterns are given in reverse, so there is no need to trace hand or tulip stems in reverse to make them appear as they do in the photo.

Garden Posies

Heart 'n Home

Pumpkin patterns are given in reverse, so there is no need to trace them in reverse to make them appear as they do in the photos.

Pumpkin Pals

Heart 'n Home

Flag Heart or Patchwork Heart

Pumpkin Pals

Pumpkin patterns are given in reverse, so there is no need to trace them in reverse to make them appear as they do in the photos.

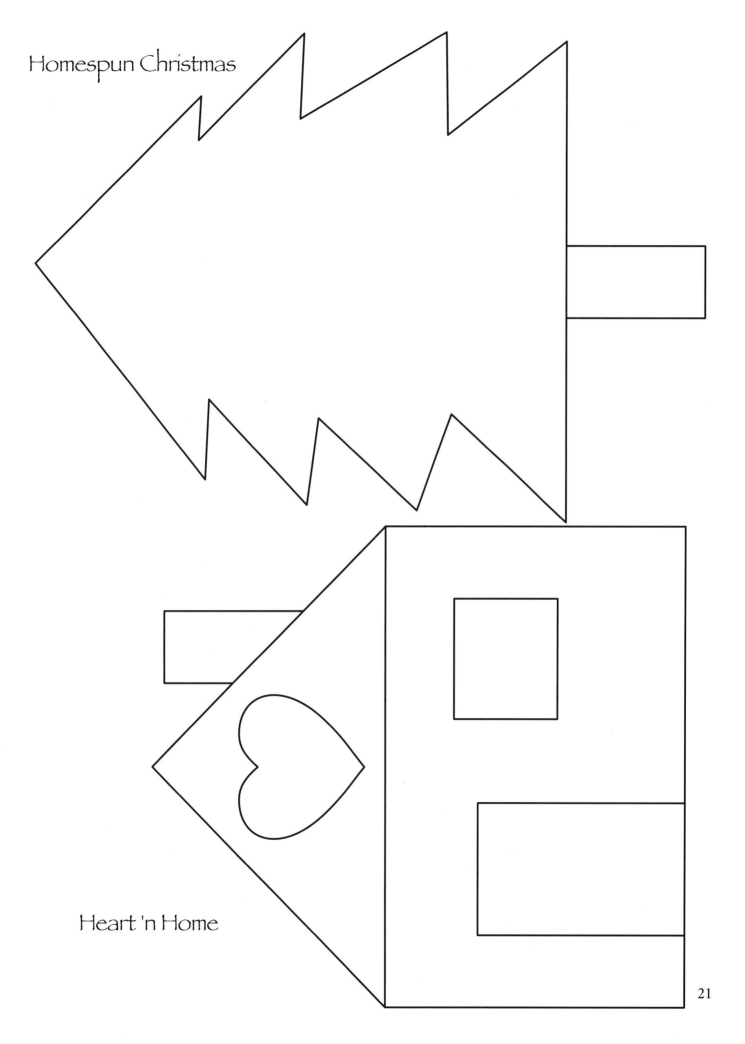

Homespun Christmas

Heart 'n Home

Homespun Christmas

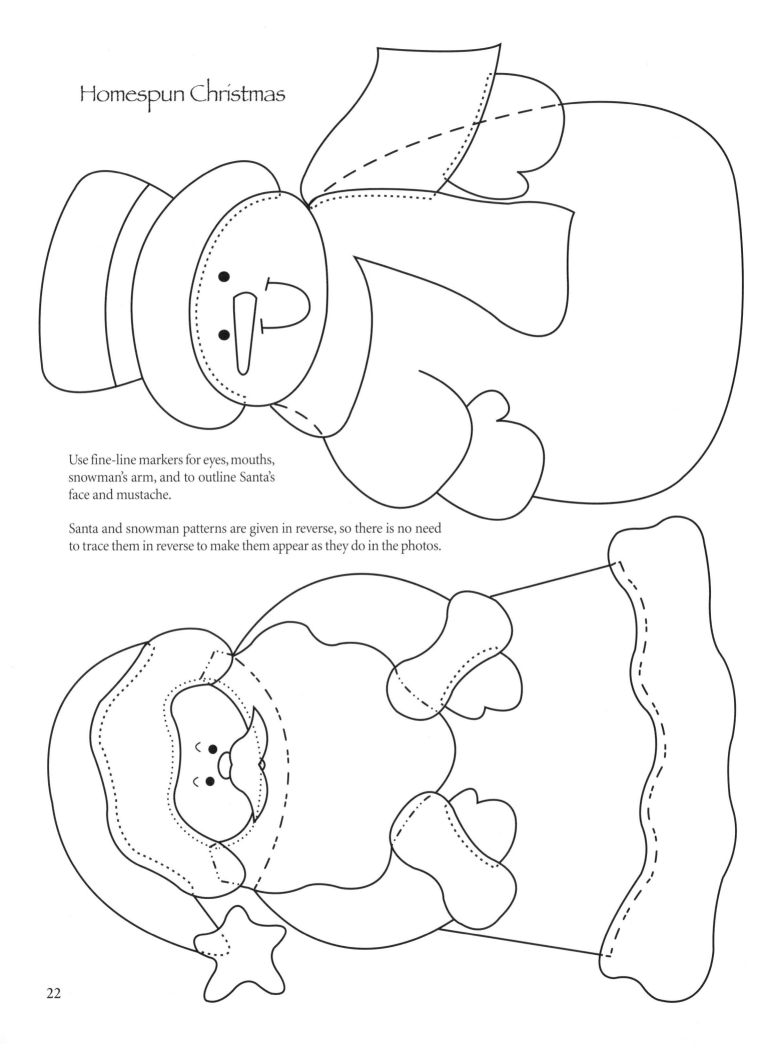

Use fine-line markers for eyes, mouths, snowman's arm, and to outline Santa's face and mustache.

Santa and snowman patterns are given in reverse, so there is no need to trace them in reverse to make them appear as they do in the photos.

Holiday Wrappings

Star and Heart

Use fine-line markers for eyes and to outline face and mustache.

Heart 'n Home

Alternatives to Buttonholes

1. Stitch buttons through both front and back pillow hems on one side of pillow. Put pillow form into pillow cover. Pin front and back hems together on other side of pillow, then stitch buttons through both hems.

2. Stitch buttons through both front and back pillow hems on one side of pillow. Hand stitch large snaps or Velcro strips to inside of front and back hems on other side of pillow. Then stitch buttons in place on top of snaps or Velcro.